# THE POLITICALLY CORRECT SCRAPBOOK

## By John and Laura Midgley

Baa Baa ~~Black~~ Multicoloured Sheep...

## Illustrated by Beverley Rodgers

# THE POLITICALLY CORRECT SCRAPBOOK

First published in 2005 by John and Laura Midgley
Trevose House, Orsett Street, London SE11 5PN

**Printed and bound in the United Kingdom**

ISBN 0-9552078-0-0
ISBN 13 978-0-9552078-0-8

Illustrations © Beverley Rodgers 2005
www.ArtistForYou.com

# THE POLITICALLY CORRECT SCRAPBOOK

No offence is intended by anything in this book.
It would be a bit rude, therefore, for anyone to take offence as they
would be stealing something which was not theirs to have!

We have used our artistic licence and although virtually everything in this book relates to political correctness there are a few pieces which perhaps strictly don't but we could not resist including them!

The actual examples included in this book come from either our personal experiences, the experiences of others or newspaper reports. To the best of our knowledge, therefore, they are a reflection of real events. We are quite sure that if one or two of the events included have not occurred exactly as described, then the way things are going it will only be a matter of time before they do!

Where pieces have been taken from outside sources and there is no known author we have indicated this on the relevant page. To the best of our knowledge, quotes are accurate and attributed to the correct source. We would be delighted, however, to dedicate previously unattributed works and/or correct the sources of quotes if necessary in any subsequent editions of this book.

If you have any examples of political correctness to share or come across any amusing pieces which are similar to those included in this book, we would love to hear from you. Please see the back of the book for our contact details.

**John and Laura Midgley**

## Thanks

We would especially like to thank our family and friends for their help and support with this book!

## Dedication

We would like this book to be in memory of two very special people who are tragically no longer with us - Roddy MacRae and Paul White. Roddy was a very dear member of our family and someone who was always enormous fun. Paul was a very good friend and regularly pontificating about something - not least political correctness. In different ways they both positively affected a staggering number of people in their all too short lives and if only there were more people in the world like them it really would be a better place. We are extremely privileged to have known them both.

In memory of

Roddy MacRae
and
Paul White

**Warning:
I am reading
The Politically
Correct Scrapbook**

Just to be on the safe side you may want to display
this warning whenever you are reading this book!

When you are finished the book you may also need to
show people the little additional warning on page 99!

# Contents

# Politically Correct Nursery Rhymes

"...and then Humpty Dumpty counted to ten and got up again."

## Humpty Dumpty

*Humpty Dumpty sat on a wall,*
*Humpty Dumpty had a great fall,*
*All the King's horses and all the King's men,*
*Couldn't put Humpty together again.*
*And then Humpty counted to ten and got up again!*

# History
### (for anyone who says the original rhyme is traumatic!)

Humpty Dumpty was in fact a large canon which was used by the Royalists in the Siege of Colchester (1648) during the English Civil War. Humpty Dumpty was located at St Mary's Church but a shot from a Parliamentary canon caused Humpty Dumpty to fall to the ground. The Royalists—'All the King's men'— attempted to raise the canon. However, because Humpty Dumpty was so heavy 'All the King's horses and all the King's men couldn't put Humpty together again!'

## Pauly Put The Kettle On

*Pauly put the kettle on, Pauly put the kettle on, Pauly put the kettle on,*

*We'll all have tea.*

*Stuart take it off again, Stuart take it off again, Stuart take it off again,*

*They've all gone away.*

# History
### (for anyone who says the original rhyme is sexist!)

The man behind "Polly put the kettle on" is thought to have had five children - two sons and three daughters. The girls wanted to play house with their dolls and the boys wanted to play soldiers.  As a ploy to get rid of the boys (so that they could play with their dolls in peace) the girls would pretend to start a game of "tea party".  One daughter (Susan) would say, "Polly put the kettle on" and the other daughter (Polly) would put the toy kettle on! As soon as the brothers left, Sukey (Susan) would take it off again! Their father put their actions into words as he found it so entertaining!

## Three Visually-impaired Mice

*Three visually-impaired mice, three visually-impaired mice,*
*See how they run, see how they run,*
*They all ran after the farmer's wife,*
*Who cut off their tails with a carving knife,*
*Did you ever see such a thing in your life,*
*As three visually-impaired mice?*

# History
### (for anyone who says the original rhyme is offensive!)

The 'farmer's wife' refers to the daughter of King Henry VIII—Queen Mary I. Mary was a staunch catholic and her persecution of protestants led to the nickname 'Bloody Mary'. The reference to 'farmer's wife' in the rhyme refers to the massive estates which she, and her husband King Philip II of Spain, possessed. The 'three blind mice' were three protestants who were convicted of plotting against the Queen. She did not have them dismembered and blinded as depicted in the rhyme but she did have them burned at the stake!

## Baa Baa Mulitcoloured Sheep

*Baa baa multicoloured sheep, have you any wool?*

*Yes sir, yes sir, three bags full!*

*One for the master, and one for the dame*

*And one for the little boy who lives down the lane.*

# History
### (for anyone who says the original rhyme is racist!)

This rhyme seems to be all about tax. Wool was big business and, in the Middle Ages, farmers had to pay tax. The tax was often paid in wool with one-third going to the local Lord— the "master"—who would pass it on to the King, one-third to the church—the "dame"— and the final third would be kept by the farmer —the "little boy". This seems to be why, in the rhyme, the wool is divided up into three bags. It is impossible to say that this is the only feasible history of this rhyme (especially when it dates back to the 1700s) but it seems the most likely!

# Politically Correct Stories

# Politically Correct Times

Philip Davies, the Member of Parliament for Shipley, mentioned his experience of political correctness in his maiden speech in the House of Commons saying, "Whoever said 'the customer is always right' never worked for Asda. I encountered the customer who accused Asda of being racist towards Irish people, because we sold 'thick Irish sausages'. Trying to persuade her that 'thick' related to the sausages and not to the Irish was beyond me."

Calderdale Royal Hospital in Halifax banned visitors from 'cooing' at new-born babies following a staff advice session which highlighted the need for respect and dignity towards patients. Signs were displayed in the hospital saying, "What makes you think I want to be looked at?".

The Director of Education at Wirral Council told staff not to describe children as gifted or talented because he thought this suggested "exclusiveness".

A long-term sufferer of heart disease who planned to bathe in maggots outside a British Heart Foundation shop was told by Hastings Borough Council that he would contravene the Authority's Animal Welfare Charter and could be prosecuted if a maggot was caused injury or unnecessary distress.

The Registrar General said that the terms "Spinster" and "Batchelor" would no longer be allowed on marriage certificates as they could not be applied to homosexuals.

Wyre Forest District Council apparently told new members of the council not to say, "Ship-shape and Bristol fashion" or "nitty gritty" as these were potentially racist phrases.

Police in Cornwall told a witness they could not use the phrase "gypsy skirt" to describe the long floating skirt that someone involved in an incident had been wearing and instead insisted that it had to be referred to as a "traveller skirt".

The Board of Visitors at Wakefield Prison suggested that inmates should no longer be addressed by their surname but as "Mr" in response to complaints that the prisoners were "being shown a basic lack of respect".

# Politically Correct Times

Programme makers at Channel 4 abandoned well known sign language gestures for fear of accusations of being racist or homophobic. Despite protests from the British Council for Disabled People, the signs for Chinese (where the index finger pulls the eyes into a slant), Indian (where an imaginary dot is pointed out on the forehead), gay (where the wrist is flicked limply) and Jewish (where the hand mimes a hooked nose) were all changed.

A police constable who stopped a man committing suicide was reprimanded for grabbing the suicidal man too tightly—despite the fact that the man was high on drugs and very aggressive.

Paintings, including the popular "The Monkey's Music Lesson" by a 19th Century French artist, on show at the Cooper Gallery in Barnsley were taken down as they were feared to be "offensive" and "demeaning to animals" because they featured monkeys in human clothes mimicking human activities.

The revised edition of the Good News bible converted the previously used system of shekels and feet to a metric system where God tells Noah to build a boat "about 133 metres long, 22 metres wide and 23 metres high" and where the giant Goliath stands at "three metres tall" and wears bronze armour that weighs "about 57 kilograms".

Staff on a training course were told that if a colleague said that he was going for a "quick half", for some "amber nectar" or for a "swift bevvy" he could well be an alcoholic.

A puppeteer in Broadstairs was rapped for portraying Osama Bin Laden and Saddam Hussein as villains in his Punch and Judy show.

The Department of Trade and Industry produced a six-page, 2,000 word document detailing the placement of every yucca plant in Whitehall.

Police spent half a day investigating a potential hate crime between two patients at a mental health unit in Isleworth after one allegedly called the other a "poof".

# Politically Correct Times

Swedish home furnishings giant Ikea came under attack for not featuring women in its instruction manuals.....by the Prime Minister of Norway.

The European Parliament was forced to withdraw its 'History of Europe' booklet which had been written for schoolchildren because astonishingly it failed to mention the two world wars under the section on the United Kingdom.

Metropolitan Police Commissioner, Sir Ian Blair, ordered the force's motto to be changed because it featured joined-up writing which, he thought, discriminated against short-sighted people.

Makers of BBC comedy shows were told to complete checklists warning managers if their programmes contained jokes or references which some people might consider offensive.

Council staff banned a woman from giving daffodils to librarians because the colour of the flowers could be construed as a sign of support for the Liberal Democrat Party whose logo is also yellow. Medway Council eventually apologised to Mrs Jewess whose daffodils had unbelievably turned into a 'political flower' - never mind football - and the flowers were allowed.

Uplands Primary School in Smethwick, West Midlands banned the marking of children's work in red pen because it encouraged a "negative approach".

Police in London were told by their chiefs that they could no longer refer to people as a "good egg" or a "bad egg". They were informed that this could be construed to be racist.

Glasgow University Conservative Students' Group were told that they could not fly the Union Flag over the University, despite the fact that the rainbow flag of Gay Pride had been allowed to fly.

A prison officer was sacked for making a remark about Osama Bin Laden, 2 months after the September 11th attacks. He joked that there was a photo of Osama Bin Laden at the bottom of the chute where he threw his keys and it was feared that three Asian visitors to the prison could have been offended.

# Politically Correct Times

Organisers of a summer fair in Dewsbury, West Yorkshire, were offered a £10,000 grant by Dewsbury West Pathfinder on the condition that Asians had to be involved to ensure that it was sufficiently "multicultural" and that they removed a beer tent in case it offended Muslims. These conditions were opposed by many local Asians who said that they had no objection to the way the event was run.

A child-minder from a village near Salisbury who had worked with children for 13 years and had an impeccable record was rebuked by an Ofsted Inspector and only given a satisfactory rating as she did not provide ethnic minority or disabled dolls for children to play with.

A group of performers were banned from calling themselves "The Freak Show", in case the name offended anyone.

The Ministry of Defence spent £40,000 on a study called 'Gendered Bodies, Personnel Policies and the Culture of the British Army' which concluded that "women have a lower physical capacity than men".

The Home Office decreed that its "Prolific and Other Priority Offender" scheme could not be shortened to the acronym "POPO" after it was discovered that this was Turkish for "bottom".

The Northern Ireland Equality Commission banned Yorkie bars from their Belfast HQ because of its "sexist" advertising slogan – "Not for girls".

Swansea Council proposed scrapping their "sickness absence policy" and calling it "minimising attendance at work" instead.

Legoland was found guilty of disability discrimination after presenting a disabled worker with a commemorative lego model of himself with his arm in a sling.

An invitation was issued for a fundraising event inviting people to come along and share a "Ploughperson's Lunch".

# Politically Correct Times

As the Queen set out on her Fleet Review and Trafalgar Day celebrations, there was a re-enactment of a sea battle (and not the Battle of Trafalgar) with a red navy and a blue navy so as not to offend the French. Vice Admiral Jacques Mazars, in charge of five French vessels which took part, said: "It's not done to put the UK from one side and France and Spain from the other, but it is done to have a common memory of what has occurred 200 years ago. It is a festival of the sea." Lord Nelson's great great great granddaughter, Anna Tribe, attacked the decision saying, "I am sure the French and Spanish are adult enough to appreciate we did win that battle. I am anti-political correctness. Very much against it. It makes fools of us."

A school which had served Islington since it was set up in 1710 was asked to drop the word "Saint" from its title by the local council in case it offended other religious groups—despite the protests of the headmaster, the teachers, the governors, most of the parents and the local Jewish and Muslim communities.

A motorist was given a fixed penalty notice for having a St George's flag sticker over the EU flag on his car number plate. In response to the police issuing the penalty notice, a DVLA spokesman said, "The regulations make provision for the voluntary display of the European flag. They do not allow for the display of any other flag or symbol".

It was proposed that the traditional term used for visitors to the House of Commons should be changed from "strangers" to something less aggressive.

A police authority said that it did not use Rover cars because buying "anything British, including British cars, was an overtly nationalist statement and could be considered offensive by vulnerable, deprived and ethnic minority groups in our society".

Schools in Edinburgh were told that the scores in football matches should be re-set to 0-0 at half time if one team was 5 goals or more ahead. Also, the losing side would be able to field two extra players in the second half.

# Politically Correct Times

Mothercare changed the ending of Humpty Dumpty on their nursery rhyme CD in case children found the original version upsetting. After the traditional ending "All the King's horses and all the King's men couldn't put Humpty together again" they added "Humpty Dumpty counted to ten then Humpty Dumpty got up again!"

A dyslexic bus driver who was disciplined for: 1) using a mobile phone whilst driving, 2) running out of fuel, 3) driving his bus in the wrong direction and 4) leaving stops early, won his case for discrimination against the bus company Stagecoach. A tribunal ruled that he had told the firm at his interview that he was dyslexic and they had failed to make reasonable adjustments (and had treated him less favourably) because of his disability.

A London taxi driver who put a sign in his cab saying "Feel free to smoke" was told to remove it on the grounds that it was an infringement of people's human rights.

A report issued by the Qualifications and Curriculum Authority instructed the exam boards in England and Wales to be "more inclusive". It said that, for example, using gambling odds as a mathematical problem could be distasteful to candidates with Islamic or other religious beliefs and said that referring to "the local doctor" as "he" was "clearly unacceptable".

Many firms stopped using the computer terminology "master/slave"—which had been described as racially and historically sensitive—and used "primary/secondary" instead.

A woman who was injured in a hit and run accident in Manchester told the police that the driver who had run her over had been "fat". She was promptly told that she could not use "words like that".

A long-standing policy of giving locals free admission to the gardens at Hampton Court came under threat because it was deemed discriminatory to other European Nationals under a European Union Directive.

A picture of a little naked Indian boy was removed from a charity photographic exhibition after one complaint was made.

# Politically Correct Times

"Somerfields" were banned from broadcasting an advert with a man who wanted to get away from his monotonous day-by-day food plan. One particular Friday (which was faggot day) he said to his wife "I've nothing against faggots, I just don't fancy them".

Posters for Galaxy ice-cream were branded racist and withdrawn as they showed four spoons with the words "eeny", "meeny", "miney" and "mo" alongside them.

Hull City Council issued a guide of acceptable and unacceptable language to councillors and staff showing that words such as "pet", "dear", "duck", "love", "infirm", "elderly" and "senior citizens" were unacceptable terms and should not be used.

A Children's Holiday Club had a pirate theme but suggested that helpers did not wear eye patches or hooks on the ends of their arms in case this caused offence to anyone who was disabled.

A group of 26 volunteers who delivered up to 9,000 meals per year to 100 pensioners were told that they should undergo police checks and specialist training in order to carry on. The group had been in existence for 37 years without incident.

Shropshire puppeteer, Ronnie Alden, was told that his Punch and Judy show was no longer appropriate for the children of Wood-side Primary School in Oswestry. Punch and Judy shows have been criticised for being too violent and for encouraging domestic violence.

A cartoon in a licensees' newspaper showing a character saying, "Yes, it must have come as quite a shock to Parisians to wake up and find Frenchmen fighting in their streets—I mean they managed to get through two world wars without that happening!" was branded "totally unfunny and potentially racist." The newspaper's editor replied saying, "..baiting the French is almost a national pastime".

Officials at the Cheddar Caves in Somerset replaced the term "Before Christ" with "Before Present".

# Politically Correct Times

The "Pocket Prayers for Peace and Justice" put together by Christian Aid included re-worded prayers. Instead of "Give us this day our daily bread", it said, "You are giving us our daily bread when we manage to get back our lands or get a fairer wage". The 23rd psalm has also been changed from, "Yea, though I walk through the valley of the shadow of death.." to "Even if full-scale violent confrontation breaks out I will not be afraid, Lord".

The Hart Male Voice Choir was told not to sing the line, "Birthday greetings, bottle of wine", when they performed Paul McCartney's song "When I'm sixty four", in case they caused offence to Jehovah's Witnesses who do not recognise birthdays.

Market stall holders in Gravesend reacted angrily when a St George's flag was ordered to be removed by market bosses. Market traders—from all back-grounds—called for the flag to be allowed to remain but a member of the management said, "I don't see any reason why it should stay up."

To ensure "sexual equality in access to goods and services", European Union officials said that advertising for male or female tenants or men or women to flat–share would be outlawed.

A cricketer had to face a disciplinary hearing and was then banned from playing for eight weeks (and his team given a six point penalty) after he jokingly suggested, in the middle of a game, that a female player should "go home and make her husband's tea".

Brian Moore, the commentator, was criticised for saying that an ineffectual blow delivered during an altercation between rugby players during the Six Nations was like a "gay slap".

The Christian Union at Hull University was told by Student Union officials that it must allow atheists to help run it, otherwise they would be breaking equal opportunities rules.

# Politically Correct Times

The Chief Inspector of Prisons said she was "concerned" to find a number of officers at Wakefield Prison wearing Cross of St George tiepins because they could be "misinterpreted" as a racist symbol.

Canon Rob Morris called for the name of a community centre in Birmingham, in the building of a 15th Century pub, to be changed from "Saracen's Head" saying it was "clearly disrespectful to another religious tradition in this city".

The Government asked British diplomats in war ravaged Afghanistan—rife with drug smuggling, land mines and poverty—to give a higher priority to "gender issues" and encourage Afghan tribesmen to have counselling to get in touch with their feminine side.

A school in Sutton changed the signs in the corridors from "No Running" and "No Shouting" to "Please Walk" and "Please Speak Quietly" as the original signs were thought to have had a negative effect on the children.

Two year old twins with Peter Pan costumes from a trip to Disneyland Paris had their little replica plastic knives confiscated by airport officials who said that all replica weapons were banned on flights in case they were a terror threat.

Religious Education teachers in Norfolk were told not to mention the "Holy Ghost" in case children found it spooky.

An artist who claimed in his brochure to have stolen 36 items from 6 different High Street shops to photograph had his work exhibited by a gallery who had received a £25,000 grant from the Arts Council of England.

A senior official at the counselling service 'Relate' said that children should be encouraged to make "Special Person's Day" cards instead of "Mother's Day" and "Father's Day" cards so as not to upset more unconventional families.

An optician in Liverpool was told that she could not advertise in the local job centre for a "hard working" receptionist as this expression could be deemed to be discriminatory.

19

# Politically Correct Times

A girl who had her hair braided was banned from classes even though others were not banned because they were of "Afro-Caribbean descent". The Headmistress of the school in question in Manchester said, "We don't allow any extreme hairstyles of any description. We are a high achieving school with high standards and we don't allow any street culture into school. However, if we didn't allow some leeway for the [pupils'] cultural and ethnic background, I think it would probably be discriminatory."

The Bishop of Hulme called for the hymn "I Vow To Thee, My Country" to be banned because he thought that it was an example of the dangerous increase in "nationalism" in Britain.

The Archbishop of Canterbury, Rowan Williams, apologised on behalf of the church for introducing English hymns to far-flung countries. He said that British missionaries should have left native populations to make up their own hymns instead of making them "cultural captives".

Police in Wales advertised a vacancy for its road policing unit saying that smokers need not apply as the post was open to "non smokers only".

Sheffield and District Football League insisted that match results should not be reported in case young players on the losing side were upset by match reports of their defeat. This move followed a 29-0 scoreline which was hailed by the local paper as "A Comprehensive Trouncing".

A row broke out when a Government funded forum for mental health patients gave its website the title "Mad for Arts".

Nuns running the Tyburn Convent in Marble Arch (built on the site of the gallows where Catholic martyrs were executed with relics from 105 of the martyrs) feared they might have to close down after they were told that, as they were open to the public, they had to find £400,000 to install lifts and ramps to meet with Disability Discrimination legislation.

A proposal to fly the Flag of St George over Rugby Town Hall was ruled out in case it was seen to be racist. Rugby Borough Council said that it might send out the "wrong message" to ethnic minorities.

# Politically Correct Times

A television presenter in Norwich e-mailed 30 primary schools in Norfolk asking them if they would be interested in a free performance of a scene from Dick Whittington at their assemblies. She called some of the schools when she did not get replies only to find that the e-mails had not got through to the schools as the filters in the computers had blocked them because of the pantomime's title.

Posters in America advertising the Beatles famous "Abbey Road" were airbrushed to remove a cigarette from Paul McCartney's hand.

The signs on the Mersey Tunnel were changed from "Manned" and "Unmanned" to "Staffed" and "Unstaffed" in case they upset women.

A headmistress of an infants' school in Batley in Yorkshire banned the book "The Three Little Pigs" to avoid offending Muslim pupils despite the fact that Muslim leaders said this was absurd.

A committee of MPs recommended dropping the word "Empire" from the honours system, doing away with such titles as "Sir" and "Dame" and having targets for the sex and ethnic distribution of honours to reflect the diversity of the UK population. The moves were to remove 'classist, imperialist and militaristic overtones' and to make them more 'inclusive' for the new century.

A lady who put a tiny Union Jack sticker which she had peeled from an apple over the EU flag on her driving licence was told that she could face prosecution for defacing Government property.

Cambridge University was pressurised to alter the tradition of posting degree results on the "wailing wall" as they had been for 300 years after 400 students signed a petition condemning this "traumatic" practice.

The Foreign Office advertised the post of Ambassador to the Vatican City saying that the job was open to all suitably qualified people "regardless of gender, marital status...or sexual orientation".

# Politically Correct Staff Party

**Subject:** Staff Party   **Date:** Monday 9am
**From:** Claire (HR)   **To:** All Staff

Dear All

The firm is celebrating its 20<sup>th</sup> anniversary next Tuesday and we have booked a room at the Plaza Hotel in town for a party starting at 7pm to include dinner and a disco. The directors are very kindly paying for the food and drinks and hope that you can come along. Please let me know as soon as possible if you can make it so that I can confirm numbers. It would be helpful if you could also indicate any dietary requirements you may have in your reply.

Yours etc
**Claire Wood**
Human Resources Manager

---

**Subject:** Staff Party   **Date:** Monday 2pm
**From:** Claire (HR)   **To:** All Staff

Dear All

I have been asked by the directors to let you know that although the firm will be paying for the dinner and drinks next week they cannot be held responsible for the actions of staff as a result of eating and drinking at the party.

All staff wishing to consume more than one glass of wine must sign a disclaimer form to exclude the firm from liability for their actions thereafter.

Yours etc
**Claire Wood**
Human Resources Manager

---

**Subject:** Staff Party   **Date:** Tuesday 10am
**From:** Claire (HR)   **To:** All Staff

Dear All

Thanks very much to those of you who have replied to my note about the office party. It has been decided that the following dances will be banned at the party in case they cause injury:

Lambada
Locomotion
Birdie Song
Time Warp
Can Can
Do The Congo

In addition, I have been asked to point out that the following songs are not meant to be taken literally:

Kung Fu Fighting
Dance Yourself Dizzy
Move Closer
Hit Me Baby One More Time
Bare Necessities
Upside Down
It's Raining Men

We will also not be able to allow the "Hokey Cokey" as this could discriminate against our disabled staff or staff with arthritic conditions who may not be able to put their "Left legs in or left legs out" etc.

Yours etc
**Claire Wood**
Human Resources Manager

Politically Correct Staff Party

**Subject:** Staff Party  **Date:** **Tuesday 4pm**
**From:** Claire (HR)  **To:** All Staff

Dear All

The directors have decided that, although there are already a number of songs which will not be played (see my last note), anyone who wishes to take part in the dancing will need to complete a further disclaimer form on the off chance that they suffer from trauma if their dancing is so bad that colleagues can't help but laugh or mock in the office.

We would obviously not condone or encourage laughter at, or the mocking of, colleagues but, as a firm, we cannot be sued should this unfortunate event take place. This will be known as "Disclaimer Form 2" and the alcohol form as "Disclaimer Form 1".

I can confirm that we will be having several Scottish dances as a member of staff is one-quarter Scottish and we wish to respect their cultural right to ethnic dancing.

We are also looking into the request to provide special Djembe drums for one of our number who is one-eighth West African but are having trouble locating suppliers.

We will continue to look into this in the interests of catering for all.

Yours etc
**Claire Wood**
Human Resources Manager

**Subject:** Staff Party  **Date:** **Wednesday 9am**
**From:** Claire (HR)  **To:** All Staff

Dear All

In light of a number of recent high profile legal cases I have been asked to request that you do not go within 3 feet of the directors at the party. This is just so that there is no doubt whatsoever about any sexual impropriety and nobody will be able to misunderstand any accidental brushes or bumps in any way.

Yours etc
**Claire Wood**
Human Resources Manager

**Subject:** Staff Party  **Date: Wednesday 10am**
**From:** Claire (HR)  **To:** All Staff

Dear All

Thanks to those of you who have pointed out the fact that I mentioned the "director distance" for the party in feet and that I should have given the distance in metric units instead. I can confirm that I have checked and the equivalent is approximately 1 metre or 100cm. I hope this clarifies the position.

Yours etc
**Claire Wood**
Human Resources Manager

**Subject:** Staff Party   **Date:** Thursday 3pm
**From:** Claire (HR)   **To:** All Staff

Dear All

We have now located a supplier of Djembe drums and the directors are delighted that we are able to have a drum circle:

*"A drum circle is simply a way of communicating by playing hand drums in a professional and supportive environment. This medium provides an opportunity for businesses to build upon existing strengths, working toward greater efficiency and cohesion in everyday practices."*

Yours etc
Claire Wood
Human Resources Manager

---

**Subject:** Staff Party   **Date:** Friday 11am
**From:** Claire (HR)   **To:** All Staff

Dear All

In addition to the ban on certain dances and the dancing disclaimer form, the directors have also decided to have a policy of "no ties" for the whole evening of the party. In the interests of equality this includes men and women.

They have also decided that there should be a ban on stiletto heels in case they cause injury on the dance floor. Again, in the interests of equality, this applies to men and women.

Yours etc
Claire Wood
Human Resources Manager

---

**Subject:** Staff Party   **Date:** Friday 1pm
**From:** Claire (HR)   **To:** All Staff

Dear All

Further to my last e-mail and the responses I have received I just want to clarify that we are not a racist firm and we do not want to ban "Thais" from our party. It is "ties" in the material sense that hang around the neck that we have decided to exclude in the interests of health and safety. Thais – and anyone of any origin of course – are more than welcome at the party.

For the record, by sending this e-mail I am in no way highlighting the issue of dyslexia which one member of our staff experiences and which seems to have caused the "Tie/Thai" confusion as this would be discriminatory. I am merely clarifying matters for all of you.

The directors have also decided that it would not be appropriate for any jokes to be told at the event which include the following:

Mothers in Law
Englishmen, Irishmen (especially Irishmen) and Scotsmen
Women (especially with regards to driving)
Essex girls

In fact it would be far better if no jokes were told at all so as to avoid any offence or misunderstandings.

Yours etc
Claire Wood
Human Resources Manager

**Subject:** Staff Party   **Date:** Friday 3pm
**From:** Claire (HR)   **To:** All Staff

Dear All

Following dietary requests from several staff, I can confirm that we have requested the following meals.

Vegetarian
Vegetarian (but eats fish)
Vegan
Halal
Asian vegetarian
Low sodium
Diabetic
Low calorie
Low protein
Atkins
No Lactose
Kosher
Gluten Free
High Fibre

If anyone has not yet told us of their dietary requirements please can they do so by Monday at the latest as we need to sort this out with the ever weary catering staff.

In addition NO DRUGS may be taken at the event. We have, therefore, cancelled the coffee order and it will not be served as usual at the end of the meal.

Yours etc
**Claire Wood**
Human Resources Manager

---

**Subject:** Staff Party   **Date:** Friday 4pm
**From:** Claire (HR)   **To:** All Staff

Dear All

We have checked with the catering staff at the hotel who have confirmed that they will not be using nuts in any of the food they serve and, to the best of their knowledge, no nuts will have been anywhere near the food which is prepared.

I know that none of you have a nut allergy but the directors asked me to check this point anyway just in case.

Yours etc
**Claire Wood**
Human Resources Manager

---

**Subject:** Staff Party   **Date:** Friday 5pm
**From:** Claire (HR)   **To:** All Staff

Dear All

It has been decided that nobody will be allowed to wear a leather jacket to the party in case this offends our vegan staff.

We have also arranged for there to be no custard at the party or paper napkins which will please those members of staff with phobias about these two particular items.

Yours etc
**Claire Wood**
Human Resources Manager

**Subject:** Staff Party **Date:** Monday 11am
**From:** Claire (HR) **To:** All Staff

Dear All

This is just to let you know there will be balloons at the party but placed extremely high up so that they do not pop and upset anyone wearing a hearing aid or bring on an asthma attack.

Should any of the balloons fall down they should not be touched as they contain helium and anyone inhaling helium would find that their voice would rise significantly and this could be offensive to people with voice tonal issues.

Yours etc
Claire Wood
Human Resources Manager

**Subject:** Staff Party **Date:** Monday 3pm
**From:** Claire (HR) **To:** All Staff

Dear All

I am sure that I do not need to say this at all but the entire event will, of course, be "No smoking". This means that you must not smoke anywhere in the hotel (including the toilets, corridors and doorways), outside the hotel or in your cars on the way to the hotel in case you leave the smell of smoke on your clothes which could upset others.

Yours etc
Claire Wood
Human Resources Manager

**Subject:** Staff Party **Date:** Tuesday 4pm
**From:** Claire (HR) **To:** All Staff

Dear All

We have now conducted a full risk assessment of the party venue and have made the following additional decisions about tonight's staff party:

- A non-slip floor is going to be placed over the whole of the dance floor.

- Cocktail sticks will be banned in case they cause injury.

- There will be no ice put into drinks in case anyone has sensitive teeth.

- There will be no candles in case these cause fires.

- There will be no disco lights in case they bring on an attack of epilepsy and no smoke in case this hurts the eyes of our contact lens wearing staff.

A "Near-Miss Register" will also be available so that if we ever organise another party in the future (heaven – or non-denominational resting place – forbid) then we will be able to take into account other potential issues in advance.

I have decided not to go to the party as it sounds like no fun at all so I hope you all have a bloomin' miserable time and choke on your water!

Yours etc
Claire Wood
Ex-Human Resources Manager

27

# Politically Incorrect Quotes

| | |
|---|---|
| I am free of all prejudices. I hate everyone equally. | **W C Fields** |
| The idea that men are created free and equal is both true and misleading: men are created different; they lose their social freedom and their individual autonomy in seeking to become like each other. | **David Riesman** |
| The worst form of inequality is to try to make unequal things equal. | **Aristotle** |
| She was not a woman likely to settle for equality when sex gave her an advantage. | **Anthony Delano** |
| All this talk about equality. The only thing people really have in common is that they are all going to die. | **Bob Dylan** |
| Women who seek to be equal with men lack ambition. | **Timothy Leary** |
| The people I'm furious with are the Women's Liberationists. They keep getting up on soapboxes and proclaiming women are brighter than men. That's true, but it should be kept quiet or it ruins the whole racket. | **Anita Loos** |
| Women's Liberation is just a lot of foolishness. It's the men who are discriminated against. They can't bear children. And no one's likely to do anything about that. | **Golda Meir** |
| Feminism is a political mistake. Feminism is a mistake made by women's intellect, a mistake which her instinct will recognise. | **Valentine De Saint-Point** |
| I owe nothing to Women's Lib. | **Margaret Thatcher** |
| The Queen is most anxious to enlist everyone who can speak or write to join in checking this mad, wicked folly of Women's Rights with all its attendant horrors on which her poor, feeble sex is bent, forgetting every sense of womanly feeling and propriety. | **Queen Victoria** |
| I don't know why women want any of the things men have when one of the things that women have is men. | **Coco Chanel** |

| | |
|---|---|
| Great things are not accomplished by those who yield to trends and fads and popular opinion. | **Charles Kuralt** |
| You get paid to impact the world, not be impacted by it. | **Mal Pancoast** |
| The opposite of bravery is not cowardice but conformity. | **Dr Robert Anthony** |
| It gives me great pleasure indeed to see the stubbornness of an incorrigible nonconformist warmly acclaimed. | **Albert Einstein** |
| Conformity is the jailer of freedom and the enemy of growth. | **John F Kennedy** |
| The surest way to corrupt a youth is to instruct him to hold in higher esteem those who think alike than those who think differently. | **Friedrich Nietzsche** |
| Our wretched species is so made that those who walk on the well-trodden path always throw stones at those who are showing a new road. | **Voltaire** |
| I cannot and will not cut my conscience to fit this year's fashions. | **Lillian Hellman** |
| Consensus is what many people say in chorus but do not believe as individuals. | **Abba Eban** |
| To me, consensus seems to be the process of abandoning all beliefs, principles, values and policies. So it is something in which no one believes and to which no one objects. | **Margaret Thatcher** |
| Principle goes out of the window as consensus walks through the door. | **Clark Vasey** |
| No great advance has ever been made in science, politics or religion, without controversy. | **Lyman Beecher** |
| It is not best that we should all think alike; it is a difference of opinion that makes horse races. | **Mark Twain** |
| What people call impartiality may simply mean indifference and what people call partiality may simply mean mental activity. | **G K Chesterton** |

| | |
|---|---|
| One of the curious things about censorship is that no one seems to want it for himself. We want censorship to protect someone else; the young, the unstable, the suggestible, the stupid. I have never heard of anyone who wanted a film banned because otherwise he might see it and be harmed. | **Edgar Dale** |
| Censorship ends in logical completeness when nobody is allowed to read any books except the books nobody reads. | **George Bernard Shaw** |
| The censure of those who are opposed to us, is the highest commendation that can be given us. | **Seigneur De Saint-Evremond** |
| A people which is able to say everything becomes able to do everything. | **Napoleon Bonaparte** |
| Every man has a right to utter what he thinks truth and every other man has a right to knock him down for it. | **Samuel Johnson** |
| At no time is freedom of speech more precious than when a man hits his thumb with a hammer. | **Marshall Lumsden** |
| The only way to make sure people you agree with can speak, is to support the rights of people you don't agree with. | **Eleanor Holmes Norton** |
| I disapprove of what you say but I will defend to the death your right to say it. | **Voltaire** |
| If the freedom of speech is taken away then dumb and silent we may be led, like sheep to the slaughter. | **George Washington** |
| How I like the boldness of the English, how I like the people who say what they think! | **Voltaire** |
| Man is always partial and is quite right to be. Even impartiality is partial. | **Georg C Lichtenberg** |
| If all printers were determined not to print anything til they were sure it would offend nobody, there would be very little printed. | **Benjamin Franklin** |
| Instead of asking, 'How much damage will the work in question bring about?', why not ask, 'How much good? How much joy?' | **Henry Miller** |

| | |
|---|---|
| No one can drive us crazy unless we give them the keys. | **Doug Horton** |
| Remember if people talk behind your back, it only means you're two steps ahead! | **Fannie Flagg** |
| To avoid criticism, do nothing, say nothing, be nothing. | **Elbert Hubbard** |
| Never retract, never explain, never apologise; get things done and let them howl. | **Nellie McClung** |
| Never offend people with style when you can offend them with substance. | **Sam Brown** |
| Whenever anyone has offended me, I try to raise my soul so high that the offence cannot reach it. | **Rene Descartes** |
| No one can be as calculatedly rude as the British, which amazes Americans, who do not understand studied insult and can only offer abuse as a substitute. | **Paul Gallico** |
| The only gracious way to accept an insult is to ignore it; if you can't ignore it, top it; if you can't top it, laugh at it; if you can't laugh at it, it's probably deserved. | **Russell Lynes** |
| Someone's opinion of you does not have to become your reality. | **Les Brown** |
| What you think of me is none of my business. | **Terry Cole-Whittaker** |
| When a person can no longer laugh at himself, it is time for others to laugh at him. | **Thomas Szasz** |
| An apology? Bah! Disgusting! Cowardly! Beneath the dignity of any gentleman, however wrong he might be. | **Baroness Orczy** |
| A true gentleman is one who is never unintentionally rude. | **Oscar Wilde** |
| It is a good rule in life never to apologise.  The right sort of people do not want apologies and the wrong sort take a mean advantage of them. | **P G Wodehouse** |
| The important thing is not what they think of me but what I think of them. | **Queen Victoria** |

| | |
|---|---|
| Nothing fails like success because we don't learn from it. We learn only from failure. | **Kenneth Boulding** |
| Ninety-nine percent of the failures come from people who have the habit of making excuses. | **George Washington Carver** |
| Our greatest glory is not in never falling but in rising every time we fall. | **Confucius** |
| You may not realise it when it happens but a kick in the teeth may be the best thing in the world for you. | **Walt Disney** |
| Failure is only the opportunity to begin again more intelligently. | **Henry Ford** |
| No man ever became great or good except through many and great mistakes. | **William E Gladstone** |
| If there exists no possibility of failure, then victory is meaningless. | **Robert H Schuller** |
| My play was a complete success. The audience was a failure. | **Unknown** |
| Winners never quit and quitters never win. | **Vince Lombardi** |

| | |
|---|---|
| No people do so much harm as those who go about doing good. | **Mandell Creighton** |
| It seems our fate to be incorrect (look where we live, for example) and in our incorrectness stand. | **Alice Walker** |
| My way of joking is to tell the truth. It's the funniest joke in the world. | **George Bernard Shaw** |
| I never drink water. I'm afraid it will become habit-forming. | **W C Fields** |
| I'd hate to be a teetotaller. Imagine getting up in the morning and knowing that's as good as you're going to feel all day. | **Dean Martin** |
| Diplomacy is to do and say the nastiest things in the nicest way. | **Isaac Goldberg** |
| A blind man will not thank you for a looking-glass. | **English Proverb** |
| He who has not Christmas in his heart will never find it under a tree. | **Roy L Smith** |
| Pull out a Monte Cristo at a dinner party and the political liberal turns into the nicotine fascist. | **Martyn Harris** |
| Common sense is the knack of seeing things as they are and doing things as they ought to be done. | **Josh Billings** |
| Common sense is in spite of, not as the result of, education. | **Victor Hugo** |
| To see what is in front of one's nose requires a constant struggle. | **George Orwell** |
| It is better to have too much courtesy than too little, provided you are not equally courteous to all, for that would be injustice. | **Baltasar Gracian** |
| I think patriotism is like charity - it begins at home. | **Henry James** |
| In the old times men carried out their rights for themselves as they lived but nowadays every baby seems born with a social manifesto in its mouth much bigger than itself. | **Oscar Wilde** |
| I have seen great intolerance shown in support of tolerance. | **Samuel Taylor Coleridge** |

# Politically Correct Trafalgar

**Nelson:** "Order the signal, Hardy"

**Hardy:** "Aye, aye sir."

**Nelson:** "Hold on, that's not what I dictated to the signal officer. What's the meaning of this?"

**Hardy:** "Sorry sir?"

**Nelson:** "It says here, 'England expects every person to do his duty regardless of race, gender, sexual orientation, religious persuasion or disability.' What gobbledygook is this?"

**Hardy:** "Admiralty policy, I'm afraid sir. We're an equal opportunities employer now. We had the devil's own job getting 'England' past the censors, lest it be considered racist."

**Nelson:** "Gadzooks, Hardy. Hand me my pipe and tobacco."

**Hardy:** "Sorry sir. All naval vessels have been designated smoke-free working environments."

**Nelson:** "In that case, break open the rum ration. Let us splice the mainbrace to steel the men before battle."

**Hardy:** "The rum ration has been abolished, Admiral, it's part of the Government's policy on binge drinking."

**Nelson:** "Good heaven's Hardy, I suppose we'd better get on with it...full speed ahead."

**Hardy:** "I think you'll find that there's a four knot speed in this stretch of water."

**Nelson:** "Damn it man! We are on the eve of the greatest sea battle in history. We must advance with all despatch. Report from the crow's nest please."

**Hardy:** "That won't be possible, sir."

**Nelson:** "What?"

**Hardy:** "Health and Safety have closed the crow's nest. No harness. They also said the rope ladder doesn't meet regulations. They won't let anyone up there until a proper scaffolding can be erected."

**Nelson:** "Then get me the ship's carpenter without delay, Hardy."

**Hardy:** "He's busy knocking up a wheelchair access to the fo'c'sle Admiral."

**Nelson:** "Wheelchair access? I've never heard of anything so absurd."

**Hardy:** "Health and safety again, sir. We have to provide a barrier-free environment for the differently abled."

**Nelson** "Differently abled? I've only one arm and one eye and I refuse even to hear mention of the word. I didn't rise to the rank of admiral by playing the disability card."

**Hardy:** "Actually, sir, you did. The Royal Navy is under-represented in the areas of visual impairment and limb deficiency."

**Nelson:** "Whatever next? Give me full sail. The salt spray beckons."

**Hardy:** "A couple of problems there too, sir. Health and Safety won't let the crew up the rigging without hard hats. And they don't want anyone breathing in too much salt – haven't you seen the adverts?"

**Nelson:** "I've never heard such infamy. Break out the cannon and tell the men to stand by to engage the enemy."

**Hardy:** "The men are a bit worried about shooting at anyone, Admiral."

**Nelson:** "What? This is mutiny."

**Hardy:** "It's not that, sir. It's just that they're afraid of being charged with murder if they actually kill anyone. There's a couple of legal aid lawyers on board, watching everyone like hawks."

**Nelson:** "Then how are we supposed to sink the Frenchies and the Spanish?"

**Hardy:** "Actually, sir, we're not. The Frenchies and the Spanish are our European partners now. According to the Common Fisheries Policy, we shouldn't even be in this stretch of water. We could get hit with a claim for compensation."

**Nelson:** "But you must hate a Frenchman as you hate the devil."

**Hardy:** "I wouldn't let the ship's diversity co-ordinator hear you saying that sir. You'll be up on a disciplinary."

**Nelson:** "You must consider every man an enemy who speaks ill of your King."

**Hardy:** "Not any more sir. We must be inclusive in the multicultural age. Now put on your Kevlar vest and life jacket; it's the rules."

**Nelson:** "Don't tell me – Health and Safety. Whatever happened to rum, sodomy and the lash?"

**Hardy:** "As I explained, sir, rum is off the menu! And there's a ban on corporal punishment."

**Nelson:** "And what about Sodomy?"

**Hardy:** "I believe that is now legal, sir."

**Nelson:** "In that case...kiss me Hardy."

**Source:** Internet—unknown

# The Sad Passing Of Common Sense

Today we mourn the passing of our beloved old friend, Common Sense, who was with us for many years. No one knows for sure how old he was because his birth records were lost long ago in bureaucratic red tape.

He will be remembered as having cultivated such valuable lessons as knowing when to come in out of the rain, why the early bird catches the worm, that life isn't always fair and that maybe it really was your fault.

Common Sense lived by simple, sound financial policies (like not spending more than you earn) and reliable parenting strategies (that adults, not children, are in charge).

His health began to deteriorate rapidly when well-intentioned but overbearing regulations were put in place.

Common Sense's condition worsened when parents attacked teachers for doing the job they failed to do in disciplining their unruly children.

It declined even further when schools were required to get parental consent to administer headache pills, sun lotion or a sticky plaster to a pupil but did not need to inform the parents when a pupil became pregnant and wanted to have an abortion.

Common Sense took a beating when it became apparent that people could no longer defend themselves against burglars who came into their houses—and got worse when it transpired that the burglar could even sue the homeowner for assault or injury caused whilst committing the crime!

Common Sense finally gave up the will to live after a woman failed to realise that a steaming cup of coffee was hot and, when she spilled a little on her lap, was promptly awarded a huge settlement.

Common Sense was preceded in death by his parents—*Truth* and *Trust*; his wife—*Manners*; his daughter—*Reason* and his son—*Responsibility*. He is survived by three stepbrothers—*I Know My Rights*, *Someone Else is to Blame* and *I'm A Victim*.

Not many attended his funeral because so few realised he was gone.

If you still remember him then try to live your life his way—the common sense way—and not allow his death to have been in vain!

**Source:** Internet—unknown (amended)

# Health and Safety v Risk

# Health and Safety Guardian

Marriot Hotels would not serve rare or medium rare steaks without their customers completing a legal disclaimer waiving the restaurant's responsibilities if they suffered food poisoning. The form also had to be signed by the chef on duty and the restaurant supervisor. "Marriot" later retracted the forms but not before they had issued a statement saying, "Customers who choose to have their burger cooked rare or medium rare do so at their own risk".

Parishioners at Sheffield's Anglican Cathedral were told that, in the interests of health and safety, when they had their feet washed on Maundy Thursday, they would all be given individual towels and would not share one towel as per usual.

Abbeyfield School in Wiltshire banned children from playing football or rugby in the playground because it was considered too dangerous.

Swimmers at a pool in Kent were stopped from doing the backstroke in case they banged their head on the edges of the pool.

Residents of Bow Quarter in East London were told that a recent health and safety inspection had identified plant pots and window boxes as a potential health risk—technically as an "avoidable event"—and, as a result, they had to be removed.

A primary school's Pancake Day race nearly had to be cancelled after public liability insurance for the event in a Devon town increased from the previous year by 400%. Underwriters also demanded a detailed risk assessment and 25 marshals to line the 80-yard route to ensure public safety.

Cycling paramedics in Norwich were told they could no longer cycle through a shopping centre on their way to emergency call outs in case they hit shoppers who could sue for compensation.

The Food Standards Agency published a six-page guide (at taxpayers' expense) on how people should wash their hands.

# Health and Safety Guardian

Schools up and down the country banned conker games after undertaking risk assessments and deciding they were too dangerous. Others banned them on the grounds that they posed the threat of a nut allergy and a school in Cumbria did not ban them but made children wear goggles when playing with them.

Health and Safety inspectors recommended that the Armed Services used chlorine to disinfect the water in an assault course and handrails to stop soldiers slipping on muddy training slopes.

The Environment Agency erected signposts along the length of the sea wall in Felixstowe warning that falling off might be dangerous.

A headmaster in Cumbria banned the use of crash mats in his school gym because he feared that they encouraged pupils to take risks.

People taking part in a traditional Christmas procession in Cornwall were forced to use glow sticks instead of flaming torches because of health and safety concerns.

The head of Whitstable Oyster Festival resigned after 10 years as Chairman when the local council asked him to complete 53 risk assessments on the event.

Saffron Walden Community Hospital in Essex banned patients eating cakes made by the local Women's Institute on hygiene grounds but reversed its decision after an outcry by the WI and the public.

Trapeze artists were told by Insurers to wear hard hats whilst performing following the implementation of the European Union's "Temporary Work at Heights" directive.

The headteacher of a school in West Yorkshire said that children should no longer bring lunchboxes into school as they were very bulky and teachers could trip over them.

# Health and Safety Guardian

The local council added a non-slip surface to the highly polished floor in Todmorden Town Hall used by ballroom dancers, in order to comply with Health and Safety Regulations.

War veterans in Walton, Essex were shocked to be told that the traditional firing of a salute to mark the beginning and the end of the 2 minute silence on Remembrance Sunday was to be banned on health and safety grounds.

Police were told that they could no longer hoist the Union Jack outside their station in Woodbridge in Suffolk because it "may be too dangerous" despite no injuries in the past 70 years.

Fife Council chiefs ordered schools, leisure centres and community centres not to allow anyone using their premises to hire inflatable bouncy castles for parties, fetes and gala days claiming they were too dangerous.

The landlord of the Woolpack Public House in Warehorne near Ashford in Kent was advised to take down the hops draped around the pub's 16th Century beams as they were seen to be a fire risk under new licensing regulations.

A headteacher banned the annual end of term rounders match between pupils and staff because of fears that there could be claims for compensation.

A boy of 11 who broke his leg in the playground was told by the headmistress of Balksbury Junior School in Andover not to return to school. She had been advised by the Health and Safety Executive that his plaster was a potential danger to other children.

Derby City Council issued guidance to schools in its area saying that they should consider cancelling trips on hot days. Teachers were not able to rub sun cream onto pupils in case they were accused of inappropriate physical contact and it was thought the children could get burnt as a result.

# Health and Safety Guardian

Poppy sellers were told not to help donors by pinning Remembrance Day poppies to their coats in case they accidentally pricked them. The Royal British Legion also asked volunteers not to put stickers on people's coats in case the stickers left marks.

Children were banned from making daisy chains at a primary school in case they caught germs or injured themselves.

After years of children being encouraged to master the art of penmanship, the risk of swallowing the cap was deemed greater than the desire for good handwriting. Waterman added a warning to their fountain pens - "These pens are not intended for use by anyone under the age of 14 years".

Swings in Wiltshire which had been in place for 25 years had to be replaced after an inspection reported that they were "too high".

Parents who got together to buy a paddling pool for children to use were told to remove it from council-owned land in Leamington Spa in case someone sued following an accident.

A hospital security guard who climbed scaffolding to save a suicidal man was sacked for "a serious breach of Health and Safety Regulations".

A local education authority urged schools to ban pupils from wearing swimming goggles in case teachers helping pupils put them on were distracted from watching the pool.

A village carnival in Totton and Eling which had run since 1912 had to be axed after someone threw a water bomb resulting in the carnival organisers being sued for "distress and pain". The subsequent increase in the insurance premium forced the event to be cancelled.

Charity shops told customers they could no longer accept electrical goods as donations to re-sell in case they were faulty and the new owner decided to sue the charity shop.

The headteacher and governors at Crudwell Church of England Primary School in Malmesbury, Wiltshire, banned children taking birthday cakes into school from home unless they were shop bought and stopped the selling of home-made cakes at its summer fete after they were told that they would be liable if anyone became ill. The County Council said that it had issued guidelines that schools should avoid selling home-made products as they carry a higher than normal risk of food related illnesses. Such foods, they said, included cream, eggs, other dairy products, fish and meat.

A British Horse Society Approved Riding School in Gloucestershire was told by its Insurers that they would be unable to renew their existing insurance policy because of the number of claims that had been received from other riding schools as part of the growing blame culture.

The temporary head-teacher of Hollybrook School near Southampton banned the annual rounders match between staff and pupils in case someone was injured and decided to sue.

100 year old flagstones at an 11th Century church in Chedworth in Gloucester-shire were ripped up and replaced in case someone tripped on them.

A girl was banned from bringing her own sun cream to school in case it sparked allergies in other pupils.

A car that was legally parked and properly taxed was towed away and crushed because the windows had been left open half an inch and this was deemed to be a fire risk as a passing child could have dropped a match inside.

Hanging baskets were banned on lampposts in Bury St Edmunds—one of the competitors in the Britain in Bloom competition—in case they were to fall on anyone's head.

Child protection guidelines required all church bell-ringers to undergo police checks at the Criminal Records Bureau.

# WARNING: There's No Getting Away From Risk

For the last year which information is available, the Royal Society for the Prevention of Accidents estimated that the following numbers of people were hospitalised following accidents whilst at home or at leisure—not even at work—by these unbelievable means...

| 902 people | were injured by | **Air Fresheners** |
|---|---|---|
| **1,046 people** | were injured by | **Ashtrays** |
| **1,251 people** | were injured by | **Baby's Bottles** |
| **472 people** | were injured by | **Bird Baths** |
| **185 people** | were injured by | **Breadbins** |
| **3,239 people** | were injured by | **Brooms or Brushes** |
| **800 people** | were injured by | **Bunches of Flowers** |
| **82 people** | were injured by | **Chopsticks** |
| **431 people** | were injured by | **Clothes Pegs** |
| **1,189 people** | were injured by | **Coat Hangers** |
| **349 people** | were injured by | **Cocktail Sticks** |
| **1,312 people** | were injured by | **Cleaning Cloths or Leather Chamois** |
| **2,768 people** | were injured by | **Clothes Baskets** |
| **349 people** | were injured by | **Dishwasher Liquid or Powders** |
| **267 people** | were injured by | **Drink Straws** |
| **205 people** | were injured by | **Dust Pans** |
| **5,945 people** | were injured by | **Flower Pots** |

| **267 people** | were injured by | **Furniture Polishes** |
| **41 people** | were injured by | **Kitchen Scales** |
| **820 people** | were injured by | **Wastebins and Wastepaper Baskets** |
| **595 people** | were injured by | **Pedal Bins** |
| **41 people** | were injured by | **Shoe Polish** |
| **82 people** | were injured by | **Stain Remover** |
| **800 people** | were injured by | **Washing-Up Liquid** |

However, even more unbelievably, the same set of statistics reveal that even the things that are supposed to make us better or safer are not necessarily without risk because...

| **718 people** | were injured by | **Bandages or Plasters** |
| **103 people** | were injured by | **Burglar Alarms** |
| **123 people** | were injured by | **Thermometers** |
| **5,658 people** | were injured by | **Contact Lenses** |
| **2,317 people** | were injured by | **Crutches** |
| **410 people** | were injured by | **Ear plugs** |
| **820 people** | were injured by | **False Teeth** |
| **2,112 people** | were injured by | **Goggles or Safety Spectacles** |
| **390 people** | were injured by | **Hearing Aids** |

# And another thing...

... there is no point wrapping yourself or your children up in **cotton wool** as the Royal Society for the Prevention of Accidents recorded that a staggering **902 people** in one year needed hospital treatment after being injured by cotton wool!

You might also want to bear in mind that filling in a risk assessment form can be a risky business! So, make sure it is absolutely necessary and that the risk you are assessing is greater than the following risk of completing a risk assessment...

# WARNING:

## RISK ASSESSMENTS ARE A RISKY BUSINESS

You get out your paper and pick up your pen (which injured 2,706 people in one year) or your pencil (injuring 3,321 people). You write out your risk assessment and if you make any mistakes you either rub them out (causing injury to 697 people) or tippex over them (causing another 246 injuries). And don't think that just doing it on the computer will be any safer (2,419 people were victims of computer injuries). When you are working out your figures you use your calculator (41 injuries) and then you either paperclip the pages together (123 injuries) or staple them (1,907 injuries). When you are finished you hole-punch the pages (41 injuries) and if you are really brave, keep them in a book or a file (4,224 injuries). If you seal up your file with a rubber band you had better watch out (779 injuries) and also be careful if you tack the assessment (308 injuries) or fix it to a wall with a drawing pin (595 injuries)!

*"The chief danger in life is that you may take too many precautions"*

# CONGRATULATIONS

**TO ALL THE CHILDREN WHO SURVIVED THE
1920s, 1930s, 1940s, 1950s, 1960s, 1970s and 1980s!**

Firstly, we survived being born to mothers who smoked and/or drank while they carried us. They took aspirin, ate blue cheese dressing and tuna from a can and didn't get tested for diabetes.

Then after that trauma, our baby cribs were covered with bright coloured lead-based paints and plastic bags did not have warnings on them to say they were not toys. We soon learned not to touch fires or walk in front of cars because we would be told off in no uncertain terms—or even smacked—if we went near them.

We had no childproof lids on medicine bottles and, when we rode our bikes, we had no helmets.

We drank water from the garden hose and not from a bottle. We shared one soft drink with four friends from one bottle and nobody actually died from this. We ate homemade cakes, white bread and real butter but we weren't overweight because we were always outside playing.

We would leave home in the morning and play all day. We would go home at night when the streetlights came on.

No one was able to reach us all day as we did not have mobile phones glued to our ears but everyone knew where we were and our neighbours looked out for us.

We would spend hours building our go-carts out of scraps and then ride down the hill, only to find out we had forgotten the brakes. After running into the bushes a few times, we learned to solve the problem.

Girls played netball or hockey and boys played rugby or football; girls wore skirts to school and boys wore trousers—none of this was considered sexist.

We did not have Playstations, Nintendos or X-boxes. No video games, no 99 channels on cable, no DVDs, no surround sound, no personal computers, no Internet or Internet chat rooms....we had friends and we played outside with them!

We fell out of trees, cut ourselves, broke bones and teeth but nobody sued anyone for these accidents.

We ate worms and mud pies (made from dirt) but the worms did not live in us forever. We played conkers, hopscotch, tag, marbles, leapfrog, British bulldog and yo-yos. We skipped, had snowball fights and went hurtling down hills in our sledges at the first sight of snow.

We had competitive sports so not everyone could win. Those who didn't win had to learn to deal with disappointment. Imagine that!!

The idea of a parent bailing us out if we broke the law was unheard of—they actually sided with the law!

These decades produced some of the best risk-takers, problem-solvers and inventors ever! We had freedom, failure, success and responsibility and we were well equipped to deal with it all.

If you are 25 or over—you are probably one of these people so why not pat yourself on the back and congratulate yourself for having survived!

If you are not yet 25—this might show you just how brave your parents and grandparents were before there was such a thing as a nanny state!

**Source:** Internet—unknown (amended)

# Politically Correct Language

| | |
|---|---|
| Blackboard | Chalkboard |
| Black Coffee | Coffee Without Milk |
| Brainstorm | Thought Shower |
| Chairman | Chair |
| Christmas Tree | Festive Tree |
| Diabetic | Person With Diabetes |
| Dinner Lady | Midday Assistant |
| Dipstick | Oil Level Indicator |
| Dyke (low wall) | Low Wall |
| Fat | Metabolically Slower |
| Guide Dog | Enabling Dog/Seeing Eye Dog |
| Lollipop Lady | Crossing Officer |
| Manhole | Personhole |
| Mankind | Humankind |
| Manned/Unmanned | Staffed/Unstaffed |
| Manpower | Human Resources |
| Naughty | Using "Challenging Behaviour" |
| Postman | Post Delivery Person |
| Toilet Break | Comfort Break |
| Wrong | Differently Logical |
| Yankee/Zulu (in phonetic alphabet) | Yellow/Zebra |

57

Future Politically Correct Sayings?

| X | √ |
|---|---|
| Love is blind | Love is sight-challenged |
| A bad workman blames his tools | A skill-challenged workperson transfers responsibility to his tools |
| There's nowt so queer as folk! | There is nothing as abnormal as normal people |
| The pot calling the kettle black | The pot calling the kettle without milk |
| Beggars can't be choosers | Wealth-challenged persons cannot make positive choices |
| If the cap fits, wear it | If the cap, turban, veil, scarf, hat or burka fits, wear it |
| Faint-heart never won fair lady | Strength-challenged heart never won woman with any colour of hair |
| If the mountain will not come to Mohammed, Mohammed must go to the mountain | If the mountain will not come to the non-denominational religious leader, the non-denominational religious leader must go to the mountain |
| A fool and his money are soon parted | A wisdom-challenged person and his disposable income are soon parted |
| It takes two to tango | It takes two to tango, waltz, jive, folk dance, rap, line dance or rave |

# Politically Correct Job Advert

**Placing an advert with the Job Centre for a vacancy can't be that difficult – can it?  This is the rough text of a real conversation that took place.**

**Employer:** "I'm calling to place an advert with you - we'd like you to find someone to fill our vacancy of office junior.  The wording we'd like you to use is - *We are looking for someone who is 20 or over*..."

**Job Centre Worker:** "Sorry to interrupt madam but you can't say that."

**Employer:** "Why not?"

**Job Centre Worker:** "Because you can't specify an age."

**Employer:** "Oh - well how about - *We are looking for someone who is mature*?"

**Job Centre Worker:** "No - you can't say that either".

**Employer:** "Oh, all right then.  Let's start again.  *We are looking for someone who is enthusiastic*..."

**Job Centre Worker:** "You can't say that because it's politically incorrect."

**Employer:** "What do you mean it's politically incorrect?"

**Job Centre Worker:** "It's just not allowed as it is discriminatory."

**Employer:** "This is ridiculous. Let's carry on then.  *We are looking for someone who can carry heavy post if necessary*..."

**Job Centre Worker:** "How heavy will the post be? How many kilos?"

**Employer** *(getting more exasperated):* "I don't know how many kilos of post there would be as it varies each day - but the person won't be able to do the job if they can't carry the post bags to the post office and they can be quite heavy."

60

**Job Centre Worker:** "I'll have to check madam - but I don't think you can say that. Please hold the line. *(Pause)* Hello—no sorry but you can't put that down as it would not be fair to people with disabilities."

**Employer:** "But they won't be able to do their job properly if they are not fit enough to carry the post...oh what's the use... *We are looking for someone who is smartly dressed...*"

**Job Centre Worker:** "I'm afraid you can't say that either."

**Employer:** "For goodness sake, why not?"

**Job Centre Worker:** "Because you can't."

**Employer:** "Well what do you suggest I say? I don't want someone turning up at work with a bolt through their nose - they will be seen by our clients and we have a reputation to uphold".

**Job Centre Worker:** "I'll have to consult my supervisor again. *(Pause)* Hello - OK you should be able to say: 'someone who adheres to the firm's dress code' - if you have to put something down".

**Employer:** "That's ridiculous - surely it goes without saying that they'll adhere to our dress code so I can't see the point of saying that. We just want someone who is smart - huh - unlike you lot who don't have to wear ties to work any more."

**Job Centre Worker:** "Sorry madam, those are the rules and that is all there is to it."

**Employer** *(getting quite annoyed)***:** "This is a farce! Well, finally, we had wanted to say - *We are looking for someone who is articulate* - unless there is something wrong with that too?"

**Job Centre Worker:** "Well, I'm not sure if it's a problem because I don't know what it means!"

61

**Employer** *(reading):* "So instead of our original advert:"

**Office Junior Wanted For Local Firm of Accountants**

We are looking for someone who is age 20 or over, smartly dressed, enthusiastic, fit enough to carry heavy post if necessary and articulate.

**Employer** *(reading in disbelief):* "We are stuck with:"

**Office Junior Wanted For Local Firm of Accountants**

Person required.

**Job Centre Worker:** "I am afraid so!"

# Politically Incorrect Europhobia

## The Dutch

Holland lies so low they're only saved by being damned!

**Thomas Hood**

A dark German, a blond Italian and a red Spaniard seldom mean well, like a Dutchman of any colour!

**Old Saying**

Dutch is not so much a language as a disease of the throat!

**Mark Twain**

## The Irish

There are over thirty words in the Irish language which are equivalent to the Spanish 'mañana' but somehow none of them conveys the same sense of urgency!

**Patrick Kavanagh**

The Irish are a fair people—they never speak well of one another!

**Samuel Johnson**

An Englishman thinks seated; a Frenchman standing; an American pacing, an Irishman afterwards!

**Austin O'Malley**

## The Germans

The German mind has a talent for making no mistakes but the very greatest!

**Clifton Fadiman**

The great virtues of the German people have created more evils than idleness ever did vices!

**Paul Valéry**

German is the most ugly language—it sounds like someone using a sickbag on a 747!

**William Rushton**

## The French

| | | |
|---|---|---|
| The best thing I know between France and England is the sea!<br><br>**Douglas William Jerrold** | There was another war-related casualty today. The French were injured when they tried to jump on our bandwagon!<br><br>**Jay Leno** | There's always something fishy about the French!<br><br>**Noel Coward** |

## The Italians

| | | |
|---|---|---|
| When an Italian says it's pasta I check under the sauce to make sure. They are innovators of the smokescreen!<br><br>**Sir Alex Ferguson** | An English army led by an Irish General—that might be a match for a French army led by an Italian General!<br><br>**George Bernard Shaw** | I saw the new Italian navy. Its boats have glass bottoms so they can see the old Italian navy!<br><br>**Peter Secchia** |

## The Greeks

| | | |
|---|---|---|
| The Greeks tell the truth but only once a year!<br><br>**Old Saying** | The Greeks—dirty and impoverished descendants of a bunch of la-de-da fruit salads who invented democracy and then forgot how to use it!<br><br>**P J O'Rourke** | After shaking hands with a Greek, count your fingers!<br><br>**Old saying** |

**SPOOF MEMO FROM THE BRITISH EMBASSY IN PARIS**

Dear Sir or Madam

Be aware that the French Government announced yesterday that it has raised its terror alert level from 'run' to 'hide'.

The only two higher levels in France are 'surrender' and 'collaborate'. The rise was precipitated by a recent fire that destroyed France's white flag factory, effectively paralysing their military capability.

It's not only the French who are on a heightened level of alert; the Italians have increased their alert level from 'shout loudly and excitedly' to 'elaborate military posturing'. Two more levels remain, 'ineffective combat operations' and 'change sides'.

The Germans also increased their alert state from 'disdainful arrogance' to 'dress in uniform and sing marching songs'. They have two higher levels, 'invade a neighbour' and 'lose'.

Seeing this reaction in continental Europe, the Americans have gone from 'isolationism' to 'find somewhere else in the Middle East ripe for regime change'. Their remaining higher alert states are 'take on the world' and 'ask the British for help'.

Finally here in Great Britain we've gone from 'pretend nothing's happening' to 'make another cup of tea'. Our higher levels are 'remain resolutely cheerful' and 'win'.

Rule Britannia!!

**Source:** Internet—unknown

## SPOOF REPLY FROM THE FRENCH EMBASSY IN LONDON

Mesdames et Monsieurs

Ze Ambassador has asked me to issue zis statement with reference to ze leaked memo as you British say - doing ze rounds - regarding our country's raising of its general terror alert from 'run' to 'hide', or 'Marche' to 'Cacher' as we say in France.

Zis was a decision made absolument by Prezident Chirac after ze flames of de fire destroyed our wonderful fabrique de blanc drapeau that was established and working non-stop since Agincourt (it is after all good to be well prepared for ze inevitable).

However, we know we can rely on our partners in ze EU to come to our aid in times of trouble. So, I am pleezed to announce today that we 'ave successfully applied for an emergency grant from Bruxelles to 'elp us re-establish our rightful place in ze world.

Ze much maligned 'C'mon—Agree Can't You All?' policy will be used to azzist in ze setting up of 500 silk worm farms to enable us to make ze biggest and best white flags for our citizens to use in times of mild concern.

We anticipate zat in five years, silk production will be enurf to replace all standard flags into a new symbol that shows, and truly represents, France in its true colours. This will be a brand new tricolour in ze colours of blanc, off blanc and blancer than blanc.

We do not believe we will be able to azzist with ze making of ze 2012 Londres Olympic flags. We will 'ave enurf silk but will not 'elp you Inglish, Rosebif-guzzling namby pamby spoil sports out of spite.

Merci et adieu

# Politically Incorrect Jokes

### The One About The Fortune Teller

There was a newspaper story about a four-foot high fortune teller who had escaped jail and the headline was, "Small Medium at Large".

### The One About The Single Mother

A journalist was interviewing a mother who had fifteen children for "International Women's Day".

"What are their names?", the journalist asked.

"Mark", the mother said, "they're all named Mark".

"But what if you want to call one in particular?", asked the journalist.

"That's easy", replied the mother, "I use their surnames."

### The One About The Blonde

Why did the blonde stare at the orange juice carton for two hours?

Because it said "concentrate".

### The One About Colour

Jane was talking to her friend Margaret and said, "All this talk about colour is ridiculous. There's nobody more coloured than people with white skin?"

"What do you mean?", asked Margaret.

"Well, white people go pink when they are hot, red when they are embarrassed, green when they are sick, blue when they are cold,  brown in the sun, orange if their fake tan goes wrong, black if they go down a mine or up a chimney and purple if they are choking", Jane said, "And you can't get much more coloured than that, can you?"

## The One About The Tramp

A tramp approached a well-dressed businessman and asked him for money for a meal.

The businessman said, "Why don't I give you a cigarette instead?"

"Because I don't smoke", said the tramp.

"Then come into this bar and let me buy you a drink", said the businessman.

"I don't drink", said the tramp.

"Well, I tell you what", said the businessman, "take my lottery ticket instead".

"I don't gamble", said the tramp.

The businessman thought for a moment, then he said, "I've got an idea. Why don't you come home with me and my wife will cook you the best meal you have ever had?"

"Wouldn't it just be easier for you to give me the money?", asked the tramp.

"Yes it would", said the businessman, "but I want to show my wife what happens to a man who doesn't smoke, drink or gamble!"

## The One About The Fairground Ride

Two gays went to the fairground. Graham said he wanted to go on the ferris wheel but Grant was too scared so Graham went on his own. The wheel went round and round. Suddenly Graham's seat was thrown off the wheel and he landed in a heap at Grant's feet.

"Are you hurt Graham?", Grant asked.

"Of course I'm hurt!", Graham said, "I went round on that wheel three times and you didn't wave once."

## The One About The Businessman With No Ears

Sadly, Peter was born without ears.

He was a very successful businessman and wanted to hire a manager to run one of his companies so he set up three interviews.

The first guy was great. He knew everything he needed to know and was very interesting. At the end of the interview, Peter asked him, "Do you notice anything different about me?" "Why, yes, I couldn't help but notice that you have no ears", came the reply. Peter thought that this man would not be right because tact was a big part of the manager's job and he did not think this applicant had been tactful enough.

The second interview was with a woman and she was even better than the first guy. He asked her the same question, "Do you notice anything different about me?" "Well", she said, "I was thinking that your hair was a bit long at the sides and it seems to cover your ears."

Peter thought that she would not be right because observation skills were a big part of the manager's job and he did not think that she had been observant enough.

The third and final interviewee was the best of the bunch. He was a young man who was smart, talented and seemed to be a better businessman than the first two put together. Peter was anxious but went ahead and asked the young man the same question he had asked the others, "Do you notice anything different about me?"

Much to his surprise, the young man answered, "Yes, you wear contact lenses, don't you?"

Peter was shocked. "How in the world did you know that?" he asked.

The young man fell off his chair laughing hysterically and replied, "Well, it's pretty hard to wear glasses when you've got no ears!"

Peter was so impressed with his tact, powers of observation and sense of humour that he hired him on the spot!

### The One About The Cow

An Englishman, Irishman and Scotsman were standing looking at a prize cow in a field. The Englishman said, "Look at that fine English cow." The Irishman disagreed saying, "No, it's a fine Irish cow." The Scotsman thought for a moment and then clinched the argument, "No, it's a Scottish cow - it's got bagpipes underneath!"

### The One About The Desert Island

Two Englishmen, two Scotsmen and two Irishmen were stranded on a desert island. It wasn't long before the two Scotsmen started a Caledonian Club and were playing bagpipes, tossing the caber and eating haggis. The two Irishmen started a Ceilidh and downed a few pints of Guinness. However, the two Englishmen went to opposite ends of the island and would not speak to each other because they had not been properly introduced.

### The One About The Brain

An Englishman had a serious brain injury and was offered a revolutionary new brain transplant. As it was not available on the NHS he had a choice of which brain to have. The specialist told him that there was an Englishman's brain which was £1,000 and a Scotsman's brain which was £2,000. The Englishman thought long and hard and then saw another brain sitting in the corner. He asked what this brain was and the specialist told him that this would be way out of his league. "But why?", asked the Englishman. "This brain is an Irishman's brain and it costs £10,000". "Why on earth is the Irishman's brain so expensive", asked the Englishman. "Well", said the specialist, "that's because it has never been used!".

## The One About Joining The Police

An Englishman, Irishman and Scotsman were all trying to join the police. Having passed the written test they all arrive for their interviews and the Englishman goes first.

The Chief of Police says, "I'm going to ask you one question. If you get it right you can start straight away and you will be on traffic duty within 10 minutes." He says to the Englishman, "Can you tell me who killed Jesus Christ?". The Englishman replies, "That's easy, Pontius Pilate." The Police Chief tells him to see the sergeant who'll get him started on traffic duty straight away.

The Scotsman then goes in and is asked, "Can you tell me who killed Jesus Christ?". "Pontius Pilate", replies the Scotsman and he too is sent off to see the sergeant to get him started.

Finally, the Irishman is asked, "Can you tell me who killed Jesus Christ?". The Irishman hesitates. He thinks long and hard. He then stands up and starts pacing the room trying to concentrate on the facts.

Then he spots the Englishman and the Scotsman outside directing traffic and exclaims, "This is totally unfair!"

"Why?", asks the Police Chief.

The Irishman replies, "Well—because they're directing traffic on their first day and I get a murder case to solve."

## The One About The Advert

A Scotsman whose wife had just died wanted to place the least expensive death notice so he went to the newspaper office and asked them to put in an advert saying, "Janet has died". The clerk explained that there was a minimum charge but for that charge he could have up to six words. So, the Scotsman added three more words and the advert read: "Janet has died. Toyota for sale".

## The One About The Sandwiches

A Scotsman, Englishman and Irishman were working together on a building site.

"Not blooming haggis again!", said the Scotsman, opening his lunch. "Blooming haggis! Day in and day out. If I have haggis sandwiches tomorrow, I'll jump off this blooming building!"

The Englishman opened his lunch. "Jam sandwiches again!", he said, "If I get jam sandwiches again tomorrow, I'll jump off with you!"

The Irishman opened his lunch. "Cheese sandwiches again! If I get cheese sandwiches again tomorrow, I'll jump too!"

The next day the three friends sat down for lunch. The Scotsman took one look at his sandwich and said, "Haggis again!" and jumped off the building. The Englishman opened his lunch and said, "Jam again!" and followed the Scotsman down. The Irishman peered into his lunchbox and said, "Cheese again!" and jumped after the other two.

Being friends, there was a triple funeral. The Scottish widow sobbed, "If only I'd known my husband hated haggis!"

The English widow cried, "If only I'd known that my husband hated jam!"

The Irish widow added, "Begosh, I just don't understand it. My husband always made his own sandwiches!"

## The One About The Son's Name

There was an Englishman, a Scotsman and an Irishman who all met up for a reunion.

The Englishman was talking about his son and said, "He was born on St George's Day so I called him George." "That's a coincidence", said the Scotsman, "My son was born on St Andrew's Day so I called him Andrew." "I don't believe this", said the Irishman. "This is such a fluke. I have a son and I called him Pancake."

## The One About The Wife

An Irishman had the flu. "Why don't you take the day off?", said one of his workmates. "But the boss wouldn't like it", said the Irishman, coughing and sneezing. "Don't worry, he's never here on Wednesdays anyway", said his workmate. So the Irishman took his friend's advice and went home. As he passed his bedroom window, he saw his boss in bed with his wife. He rushed back to the office and said to his mate, "That was a close one, to be sure - I nearly got caught!"

## The One About Nature

A doctor was explaining to an Irishman how nature adjusted for some physical disabilities.

"For example", said the doctor, "if a man is blind he develops a keen sense of touch. If he is deaf, he develops his other senses."

"Oh, I know exactly what you mean", said the Irishman, "I've noticed that if a bloke has one short leg, then the other one is always a bit longer."

## The One About The Crocodiles

An Englishman, Irishman and Scotsman were trying to escape cannibals in Africa when they came to crocodile-infested water which they had no choice but to cross. The Irishman went first and thrashed his way to the other side as quickly as he could but he got one arm bitten off by a crocodile. The Scotsman went next and, although he was even quicker than the Irishman, he lost an arm and a leg to the crocodiles.

The Englishman seemed quite unfazed by it all and nonchalantly sauntered up to the edge of the water, swam peacefully across at a slow pace and got out the other side without a single scratch. Both the Scotsman and the Irishman looked at the Englishman in disbelief. "How on earth did you manage that", stuttered the Scotsman. "Well", said the Englishman, "I knew I was safe wearing this T-Shirt you leant me last week with the words, 'Scotland for the World Cup' on the back—even the crocodiles wouldn't swallow that!"

# Politically Correct Christmas

# Christmas Crackers

The Royal Hospital for Sick Children banned the distribution of a Christmas CD (given to the hospital to cheer up the sick children) on the grounds that it mentioned baby Jesus and could offend those of a non-Christian faith.

A man in Bedfordshire was told that he could not take a photograph of his son in his Christmas play in case he was a paedophile.

Children at a school in Gloucestershire were told that they could not wear tinsel at their school Christmas party as they could strangle themselves.

Santa was banned from arriving on water skis at Wells Harbour, Norfolk, because he would break the 3mph speed limit.

A council in Suffolk planned to scrap grants for festive lights because Christmas did not fit with its "core values of equality and diversity".

A nationwide poll revealed that a quarter of schools would not hold carol services and that a seventh would not have any form of nativity play—not even a politically correct version!

Father Christmas was banned from two units at a hospital in Leicester after hospital bosses said that having Santa visit elderly dementia patients would be like treating them as children.

Two out of three firms do not put up Christmas trees or decorations around the festive period for fear of offending non-Christians.

Scottish Parliament officials ruled that the words "Merry Christmas and a Happy New Year" should not appear on cards sent by Members of the Scottish Parliament or staff as they were not "socially inclusive".

A man was told that the tree erected in December at his workplace could not be referred to as a "Christmas Tree" and that it had to be called a "Festive Tree".

Ellesmere Chamber of Commerce used the term "Winter Festival" to describe the Christmas celebrations in the town.

Buckinghamshire Council refused to allow posters advertising carol concerts to be displayed in its libraries in case the "religious content" offended non-Christians.

# Christmas Crackers

Officials at the Department of Culture, Media and Sport sent out Christmas cards with the message "Season's Greetings" in case mention of Christmas should offend religious minorities.

A committee of the Church of England said that the Three Wise Men who brought the gold, frankincense and myrrh to the infant Jesus may not have been particularly wise and could have been women.

The Red Cross banned traditional Christmas cards from their shops saying it wanted to preserve its long-established reputation for impartiality.

A shopping centre re-named its Christmas lights "Luminos".

The TUC and the Royal Society for the Prevention of Accidents produced a Christmas safety guide for office parties which included recommendations like:

1. Leave out the mistletoe (and not just because the berries are poisonous!).

2. If you are going to be serving alcohol at the party make sure you have read your company's alcohol policy.

3. Use paper cups so that there's no danger from broken glasses.

4. Party balloons can cause severe reactions in people who are allergic to latex.

5. Resist the temptation to photocopy parts of your anatomy—if the copier breaks you'll be spending Christmas with glass in some painful places.

A survey revealed that 80% of firms in the UK would not hold a Christmas Party for fear of being sued—either for injuries caused, bad behaviour or sexual harassment.

A school in Luton instructed parents not to bring in video cameras to the nativity play in case the pictures fell into the wrong hands.

A supermarket which scoured Britain in search of lucky sixpences was told that it could not insert the old coins into their puddings because they "constituted a choking hazard".

An official at Lambeth Council called the Borough's Christmas Lights "Winter Lights" but the name was changed back after a public outcry.

## WARNING:

## Mary and Joseph—
## how it could have been!

On their way to Bethlehem, Mary and Joseph – weary and exhausted – were accosted by an overzealous traffic policeman who jumped out from behind the bushes and demanded to know what speed they thought they were doing on their donkey. As they clearly had no idea he proceeded to read from his speedometer telling them with great delight that they were exceeding the legal limit by 1¼ miles per hour.

The traffic policeman could not hide his excitement at meeting yet another target as he promptly issued them with a Fixed Penalty Notice.

Despite their protestations that this really was an emergency, he then pointed out that Mary was not wearing a riding hat which conformed to the PAS 015 or EN 1384 riding hat standards.

When he then demanded to see an up-to-date horse passport for their donkey, and neither Mary nor Joseph could oblige, he thought all his Christmases had come at once and confiscated the donkey.

Heavily pregnant, Mary was then forced to walk the rest of the way to Bethlehem.

Mary and Joseph were both quite upset as the reason they were traipsing all the way back to Bethlehem in the first place, at this most inconvenient time, was to pay their taxes. When they thought that this sort of bureaucracy was what their money was being spent on – well, it did not make them thrilled to bits shall we say!

After arriving in Bethlehem and finding that all the inns were full, they stumbled upon a very nice inn-keeper willing to put them in the stable. Just as he was about to agree to let them stay, the inn-keeper had a horrible flashback to the Health and Safety inspection he had just experienced the week before. He also then remembered that he had to bear in mind he was not allowed to discriminate against travellers so—torn between two competing laws as he frequently was—he decided, on balance, to let them in. But he made sure he told Mary and Joseph that they would not be able to use candles for light as the candles represented a fire hazard.

Then the wise men heard about the birth of Jesus over the internet and looked up the stable address on their journey planner. After a lot of dithering around they set off, bearing the gifts they had bought on eBay. However, they weren't actually all that wise because, in the interests of equality and in order to be representative, they were all intellectually-challenged. They were very late and not a lot of use and it was, in fact, a miracle they turned up at all!

A risk assessment was carried out on the gold, frankincense and myrrh. They all failed and were taken away to be re-sold on eBay. Then, the social worker (who had been called following the birth) confiscated the beautifully handcrafted toys that Joseph had painstakingly made especially for the new baby saying that they were politically incorrect, sexist and not diverse enough.

Finally, Mary and Joseph went to register the birth of Jesus at the local registry office and even this simple procedure turned into a bit of an episode. Mary and Joseph were told that they could not use the term "Christian name" on the birth certificate in case this caused offence. Then the registrar laughed out loud when Mary said that God was the father muttering under his breath, "I've heard that a few times before!"

So, it is a blessing that Jesus was born 2,000 years ago and not now as it could have all been so different!

**MESSAGE:**

# "Merry Christmas and a Happy New Year"

**TERMS AND CONDITIONS, DISCLAIMER AND LEGAL INFORMATION TO ACCOMPANY MESSAGE:**

From me ("the wishor") to you ("the wishee").

Please accept without obligation, implied or implicit, as laid down in EU Doc 324/Bs/oo-agh/2004, my best wishes for a low stress, non-addictive, gender neutral, health conscious celebration of the winter solstice holiday, practiced within the most enjoyable traditions of the religious persuasion of your choice, or secular practices of your choice, with respect for the religious/secular persuasions and/or traditions of others, or their choice not to practice religious or secular traditions at all.

I wish you a financially successful, personally fulfilling and medically uncomplicated recognition of the onset of the generally accepted calendar year but with due respect for the calendars of choice of other cultures or sects and having regard to the race, creed, colour, age, physical ability, religious faith, choice of computer platform or sexual preference of the wishee.

By accepting this greeting you are bound by these terms as passed by EU Doc 324/Bs/ee.bi.gum - that:

This greeting is subject to further clarification or withdrawal at the will of EU sub-committee Doc 324/Bs/ohh.dea.ray.me

This greeting implies no promise by the wishor to actually implement any of the wishes to the wishee nor implied to any co-workers or friends of family of the wishee who have sighted or been handed this document whether by accident or on purpose.

Contd...

**Contd...**

This greeting may not be enforceable in certain jurisdictions and/or the restrictions herein may not be binding upon certain wishes in certain jurisdictions.  This greeting is also revocable at the sole discretion of the wishor or his delegated proxy.

This greeting is warranted to perform as reasonably may be expected within the usual application of good tidings, for a period of one year or until the issuance of a subsequent greeting, whichever comes first.

The wishor warrants this greeting only for the limited replacement of this wish or issuance of a new wish at the sole discretion of the wishor or his delegated proxy.

Any indirect references you may glean from this message via word associations—e.g. "the Lord", "Father Christmas", "Our Saviour", "Rudolph the red-nosed reindeer" or any other festive figures, adornments or associated period paraphernalia, whether actual or fictitious, dead or alive, shall not imply any endorsement by or from them in respect of this greeting and all proprietary rights in any referenced third party names and images are hereby acknowledged, without favour or suffrage.

**Source:** Internet—unknown (amended)

# Compensation Claims v Warnings

**WARNING**

"This Section May Cause Amusement!"

# Compensation Chronicle

**A** woman sued her employer for supplying alcohol at an office Christmas party as she was stopped and breathalysed on the way home in her car.

**A** couple in Plymouth demanded compensation from a local supermarket after their dog injured itself jumping to grab a promotional leaflet put through their letterbox.

**A** career criminal was awarded £248,000 in compensation for a freak fall in a prison shower. Despite never having had a job in his life, the compensation payment included a substantial amount for "lost earnings".

**A** woman fell over a child in a shop in America and successfully sued the shop for her injuries. The child was her own!

**A** customer who burnt her mouth on a cup of coffee sued "McDonalds" because the contents were hot.

**A** convict in Bolton sued his Local Education Authority for failing to give him a suitable education thereby leading him into a life of crime.

**A** man who had drunk 10 pints of lager and fell over whilst changing a lightbulb was awarded £75,000 compensation because his council had, apparently, been "negligent" by installing a light fitting on a landing over a top step.

**A** woman sued a small shop and put it out of business after her child, who was roller skating around the shop, hit the door.

**A** chef who cut his little finger whilst preparing an avocado sued his former hotelier employers for £25,000, claiming they should have warned him that the avocado was unripe and consequently dangerous to slice.

**A** man sued his company because he fell over at a work social event and sprained his wrist. It was deemed not to be his fault as the company had provided a free bar which had led him to be drunk and consequently to fall over.

**A** convicted armed robber who was secretly filmed by police was awarded £1,000 in compensation when the European Court of Human Rights in Strasbourg ruled that his right to a private life had been breached by the police.

**WARNING**

Whilst we have personally seen most of these warnings there are a few (which we could not resist including) that come from the internet via www.mlaw.org.

**WARNING**

**Pint of milk:**
"Contains milk"

**WARNING**

**Artificial Nail Glue:**
"In case of eye contact, do not use acetone or nail varnish remover"

**WARNING**

**Children's Cough Medicine:**
"Do not drive a car or operate machinery after taking this medication"

**WARNING**

**Shampoo:**
"This is not food"

**WARNING**

**Tiny Air Filled Packing Bag:**
"Not a toy. Not a flotation aid. Not a pillow."

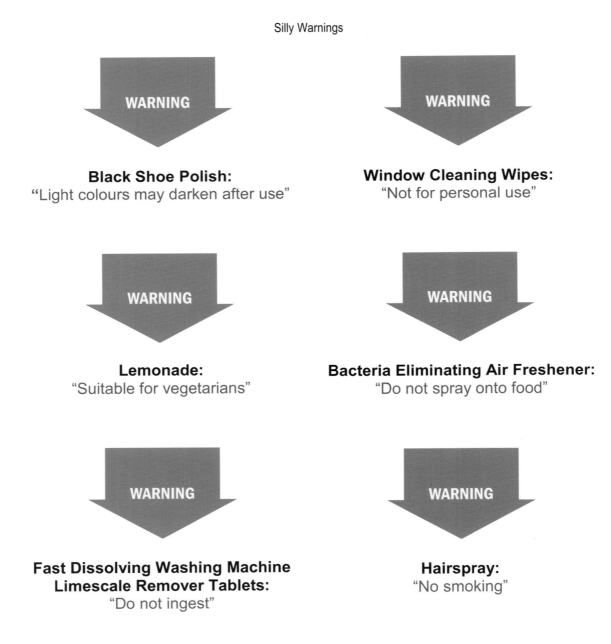

**Black Shoe Polish:**
"Light colours may darken after use"

**Window Cleaning Wipes:**
"Not for personal use"

**Lemonade:**
"Suitable for vegetarians"

**Bacteria Eliminating Air Freshener:**
"Do not spray onto food"

**Fast Dissolving Washing Machine
Limescale Remover Tablets:**
"Do not ingest"

**Hairspray:**
"No smoking"

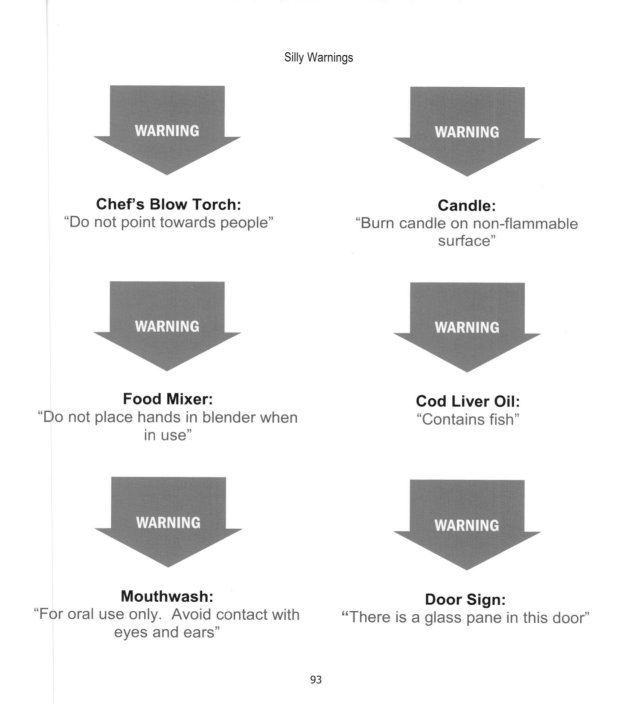

**Chef's Blow Torch:**
"Do not point towards people"

**Candle:**
"Burn candle on non-flammable surface"

**Food Mixer:**
"Do not place hands in blender when in use"

**Cod Liver Oil:**
"Contains fish"

**Mouthwash:**
"For oral use only. Avoid contact with eyes and ears"

**Door Sign:**
"There is a glass pane in this door"

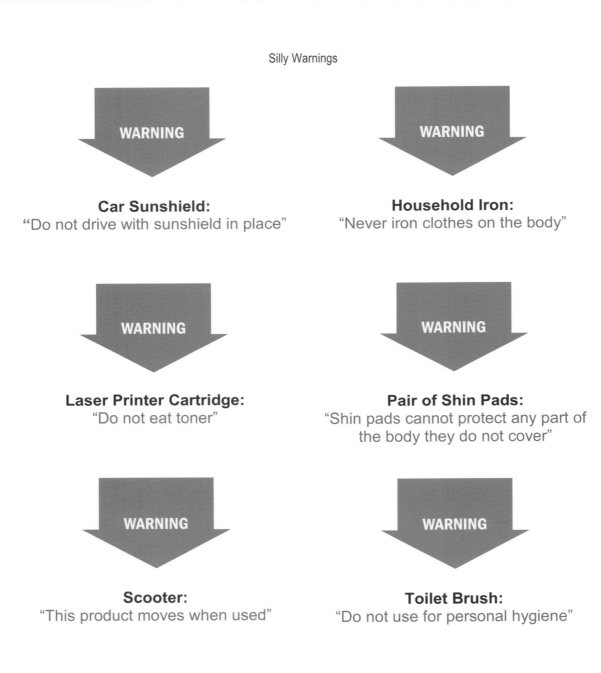

**Car Sunshield:**
"Do not drive with sunshield in place"

**Household Iron:**
"Never iron clothes on the body"

**Laser Printer Cartridge:**
"Do not eat toner"

**Pair of Shin Pads:**
"Shin pads cannot protect any part of
the body they do not cover"

**Scooter:**
"This product moves when used"

**Toilet Brush:**
"Do not use for personal hygiene"

**Child's Buggy:**
"Remove child before folding"

**Hand-held Massager:**
"Do not use while sleeping or unconscious"

**Child's Superman Costume:**
"Wearing this garment does not enable you to fly"

**Vacuum Cleaner:**
"Do not use to pick up anything which is currently burning"

**13-inch Wheelbarrow:**
"Not intended for motorway use"

**A 12 inch CD Rack:**
"Do not use as a ladder"

If this book has made you want to do something to stop the advance of Political Correctness (PC), there is plenty that can be done!

Those who push PC often have very good intentions but they need to realise that they are doing so much damage. You can actually achieve a great deal by personally challenging PC whenever you see or hear it.  However, if you are not in a position to do this, why not contact the **Campaign Against Political Correctness** and let them do it for you?

For further ideas about helping to put an end to PC, to see many more stories and examples of PC, to sign a petition against PC or to buy merchandise to show your opposition to PC you can contact the **Campaign Against Political Correctness** on any of the following:

**Website:**
**www.CAPC.co.uk**

**Address:**
**Campaign Against Political Correctness**
**Trevose House, Orsett Street,**
**London SE11 5PN**

**e-mail:**
**info@capc.co.uk**

If you would like to join the **Campaign Against Political Correctness** or make a donation now just send your details to the above address.  There is no minimum membership fee.  *Any cheques should be made payable to 'CAPC'.*  At the time of writing, anyone paying a membership fee of £20 or over (£30 or over for a couple) will receive a complimentary lapel badge.

**WARNING:**
**I have read**
**The Politically**
**Correct Scrapbook**

We hope that you have enjoyed this little book and that it has managed to raise a smile or two! Political Correctness is of great concern as it can put people off doing good deeds - for fear of repercussions or due to the volume and cost of the associated bureaucracy - and it can also seriously damage your sense of humour. So, we very much hope you will continue to treat others as you would like to be treated yourself and continue to laugh as much as you can! It is worth remembering that actions really do speak louder than words.

John and Laura Midgley